D1613637

The Robotx

Get Help from
Simple Machines

Pulling Up

The Pulley

Written by Gerry Bailey   Illustrated by Mike Spoor

Get Help from
Simple Machines

Crabtree Publishing Company
www.crabtreebooks.com
1-800-387-7650

PMB 59051, 350 Fifth Ave.
59ᵗʰ Floor,
New York, NY 10118

616 Welland Ave.
St. Catharines, ON
L2M 5V6

Published by Crabtree Publishing in 2014

Author: Gerry Bailey
Illustrator: Mike Spoor
Editor: Kathy Middleton
Proofreader: Crystal Sikkens
End matter: Kylie Korneluk
Production coordinator and
   Prepress technician: Ken Wright
Print coordinator: Margaret Amy Salter

Photographs:
All images are Shutterstock.com unless
otherwise stated.
Pg 8 – Flegere
Pg 13 – loraks
Pg 18/19 – Alvov
Pg 19 – mutation
Pg 21 – Jeff Whyte
Pg 22 – Wallace Weeks
Pg 25 – Don Tran

Printed in Canada/022014/MA20131220

Library and Archives Canada Cataloguing in Publication

Bailey, Gerry, author
        Pulling up : the pulley / written by Gerry Bailey ; illustrated by
Mike Spoor.

(The robotx get help from simple machines)
Includes index.
Issued in print and electronic formats.
ISBN 978-0-7787-0417-1 (bound).--ISBN 978-0-7787-0423-2 (pbk.).--
ISBN 978-1-4271-7535-9 (pdf).--ISBN 978-1-4271-7529-8 (html)

        1. Pulleys--Juvenile literature. I. Spoor, Mike, illustrator
II. Title.

TJ1103.B35 2014   j621.8   C2013-908711-7
                                         C2013-908712-5

Library of Congress Cataloging-in-Publication Data

CIP available at Library of Congress

Contents

The Robotx

Meet   and
RobbO

RobbEE

The robots' workshop

Usually, RobbO and RobbEE like to make NEW, useful machines in their workshop.

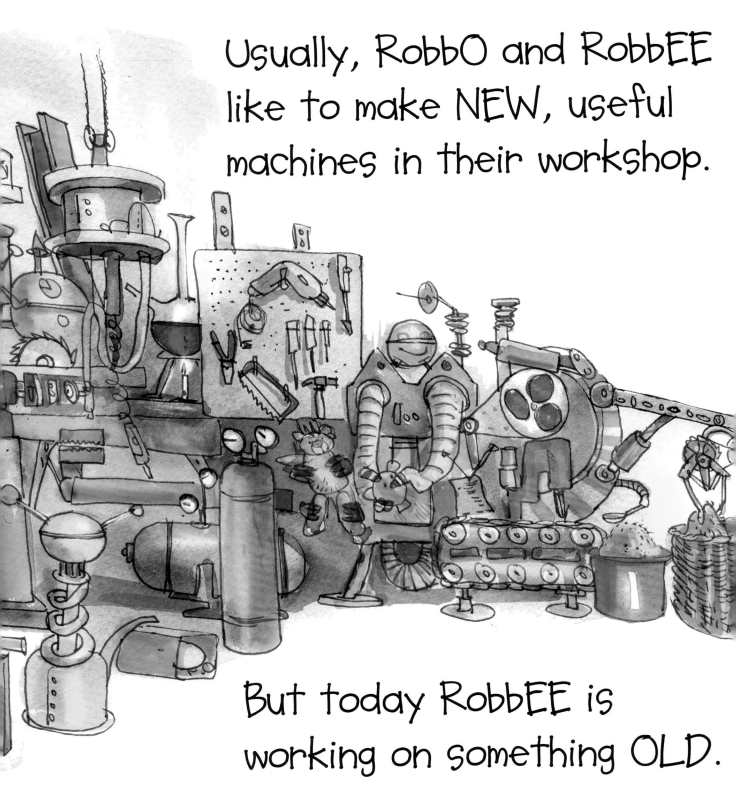

But today RobbEE is working on something OLD.

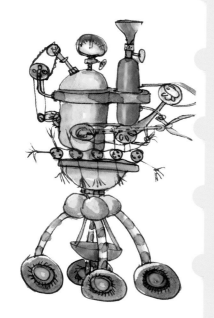

A machine is...

A machine is a tool used to make work easier. Work is the effort needed to create force. A force is a push or pull on an object. Machines allow us to push, pull, or lift a heavy weight much easier, or using less effort. All machines are made up of at least one **simple machine**.

There are six kinds of simple machines. Some have just one part that moves. Others are made up of two or more parts. The six simple machines are:

- **lever**
- **pulley**
- **inclined plane**
- **wheel and axle**
- **wedge**
- **screw**

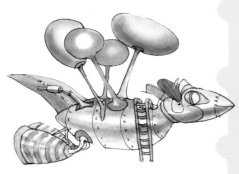

In this book, the Robotx will help us learn all about the pulley.

5

RobbEE has bought a very old car. He wants RobbO to help him get it working. First he will have to put a new engine in.

That means getting the old one out—and it's heavy! Even together the robots aren't able to lift it.

They need some help, and RobbO knows how to get it.

"We need a pulley," he says. "It's a rope wrapped around a wheel. A pulley is used to help lift things up and set them down."

"The rope fits into a groove around the wheel."

RobbO attaches the pulley to a beam above the car's engine.

They attach one end of the rope to the engine and then they pull on the other end.

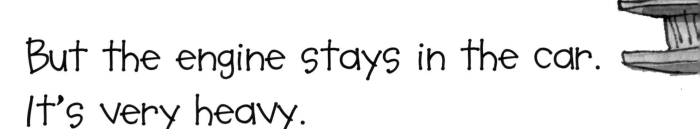

But the engine stays in the car. It's very heavy.

"We can make it easier to lift if we add a second pulley," says RobbO. "We'll add it below the one attached to the beam. Then we'll attach the second pulley to the engine."

"If this doesn't work, we just have to keep adding pulleys. The more we add, the easier it gets."

They pull again!

11

Now the old car's engine starts to rise. It swings high in the air, and the two Robotx bring it safely down to the workshop floor.

Success!

The pulley inside

Many pulleys are used in car engines. They are connected to each other by a belt. The pulley is used to move power from one place to another.

Pulleys help other engine parts create **electricity** for the car and keep the engine from overheating.

How pulleys work

A pulley is one of the six amazing simple machines. It is used to lift objects and also to set things down. It makes moving heavy objects easier.

A single pulley is a wheel with a groove in its **rim**. A rope or metal cable passes through the groove.

More than one pulley is called a block and tackle. The pulleys are the blocks, and the rope or cable is the tackle.

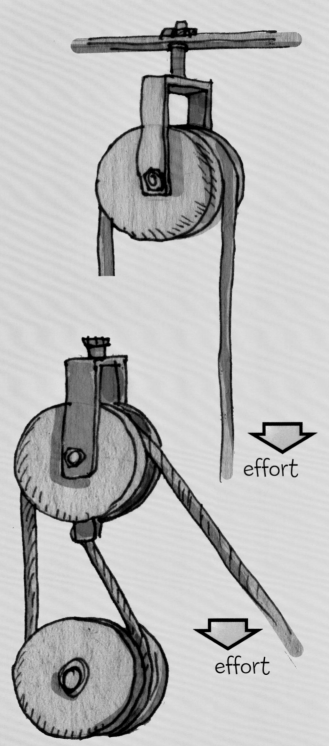

effort

effort

The more pulleys you have in the block and tackle the less effort you'll need to lift something.

Each pulley reduces the effort you need to use.

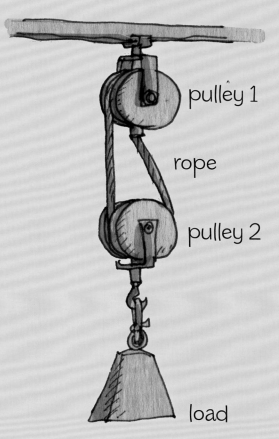

pulley 1

rope

pulley 2

load

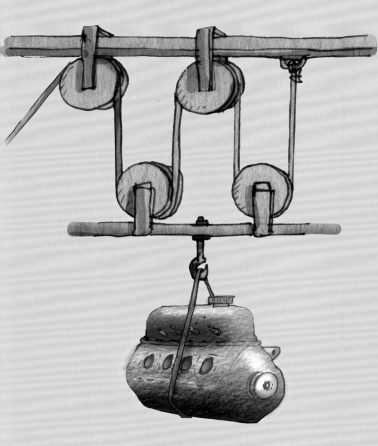

If you had four pulleys, you'd need four times less effort to lift the object, or load. But the load would only move one fourth of the distance that the rope is pulled.

An impossible load

The Robotx take a break. RobbO tells his friend a story about the strength of pulleys.

Archimedes was a great **mathematician** and **inventor** who lived more than 2,000 years ago in the city of Syracuse on the island of Sicily, which was then part of ancient Greece.

Archimedes had once said in a letter to King Hieron that he could move any weight by using enough pulleys. He even bragged that he could move the entire world! The king challenged him to move a ship full of men from land into the sea.

On the day of the event, a large ship was loaded with men and **cargo**. Everyone watched as Archimedes pulled on a rope a distance away from the ship. Slowly he drew the ship across the sand as smoothly and evenly as if it had been in the water.

Pulleys at sea

A pulley system is used on sailboats and ships to lift the heavy sails.

Different kinds of block and tackle systems are used. Some change the direction a rope is moving, while others make lifting easier.

Blocks were originally made of wood or metal. Modern ones are often made of stainless steel or reinforced plastic.

A wooden block and tackle hauls the sails on this boat.

A ship's sails are hauled into place using pulley systems.

Pulleys up high

Pulleys are often used to raise loads to a higher level.

Flagpole

Flags that fly from the top of tall flagpoles are raised with the help of a pulley system.

A pulley is attached to the top of the flagpole. A loop of rope or cable wraps around the pulley wheel. When the rope is pulled, the flag attached to it is raised.

Hoist

Painters and window cleaners have a difficult job keeping **skyscrapers** looking good.

Workers hook onto pulleys located along the edge of the roof. By pulling on the ropes, they can hoist themselves up and down the sides of the building.

More pulleys up high

Crane

Cranes lift really heavy loads. The pulley is placed at the end of its arm.

The arm acts as a lever. In this way the crane is really two simple machines working together—a pulley and a lever.

Elevator

An elevator is raised and lowered using strong steel cables. These are wound around large pulleys at the top and bottom of the elevator shaft in a loop.

A motor powers the top pulley. A heavy chunk of metal, called a counterweight, hangs on one side of the loop. The elevator hangs on the other side.

The downward pull of the counterweight helps pull the elevator upward.

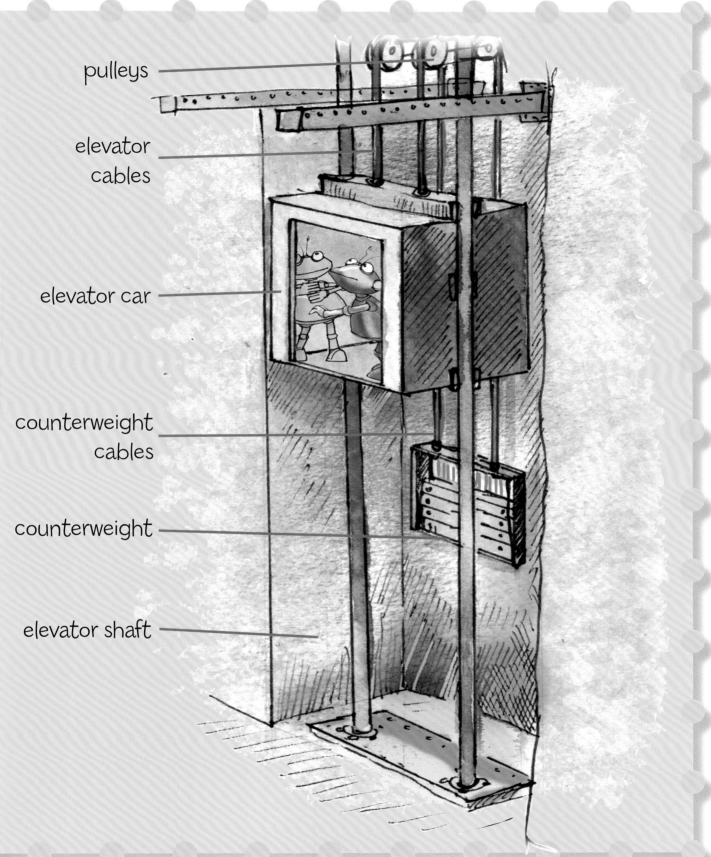

pulleys

elevator cables

elevator car

counterweight cables

counterweight

elevator shaft

23

On the ski lift

The Robotx have been busy all day using a pulley to get the new car engine in place. Now they want to go for a walk in the mountains. They are using a pulley on a ski lift to climb the mountain.

Heavy cables link their chair to the winding machinery at the bottom of the slope. Their chair runs along the cable on a smaller pulley.

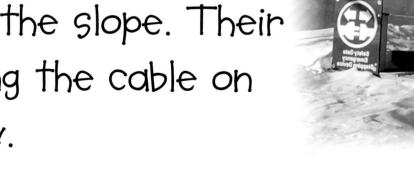

Helicopter rescue!

While RobbO and RobbEE were walking in the mountains they hear a cry for help. It's a climber who has fallen and hurt his leg.

Luckily, the rescue helicopter is on its way. Slowly it lowers a sling, which the two Robotx help put around the injured man. The helicopter uses a pulley to hoist him up to safety. Then, the helicopter heads for the hospital.

RobbO explains the pulley to his friends.

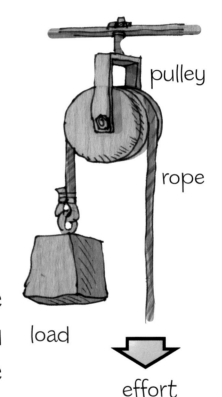

pulley

rope

load

effort

A single pulley is usually called a fixed pulley because the pulley is attached to something.

The heavy load to move is attached to one end of a rope. The rope is fed through the pulley. You provide the effort by pulling on the other end of the rope.

A single pulley doesn't reduce the effort needed, but it is easier to pull sideways or down than it is to lift up.

Another kind of pulley is called a compound pulley. It's made of two or more pulley wheels. It is known as a block and tackle.

If you pull the rope down 10 inches (25.4 cm), the load is lifted only half that distance— 5 inches (12.7 cm). But it takes only half the effort to do it.

Build a muscle builder

The Robotx think of another clever use for a pulley. RobbEE invents an exercise machine to help make their muscles strong.

Exercise machines use pulleys. These control the angle at which the weights will be lifted.

Using pulleys in this way makes lifting weights safer, as well as more useful in helping to build muscle!

Learning more

Books

Put Pulleys to the Test
By Roseann Feldman and Sally M. Walker
(Lerner Publishing Group, 2011)

Simple Machines: Pulleys
By Valerie Bodden
(Creative Paperbacks, 2011)

How Toys Work: Pulleys
By Sian Smith
(Heinemann, 2012)

Websites

www.mocomi.com/pulley/
An animated clip describing what a pulley is and how it is used.

teacher.scholastic.com/dirtrep/simple/pulley.htm
A short summary on how a pulley works.

www.mikids.com/SMachinesPulleys.htm
Examples of pulleys and how they are used.

Glossary

cargo Materials or goods

electricity A form of energy which powers machines to work

inclined plane A slanted surface connecting a lower point to a higher point

inventor A person who creates things

lever A bar that rests on a support called a fulcrum which lifts or moves loads

mathematician A person who is very good at math

pulley A simple machine that uses grooved wheels and a rope to raise, lower, or move a load

rim The outer edge of something

screw An inclined plane wrapped around a pole which holds things together or lifts materials

simple machine A machine that makes work easier by transferring force from one point to another

skyscrapers Tall buildings

wedge Two inclined planes joined together used to split things

wheel and axle A wheel with a rod, called an axle, through its center which lifts or moves loads

Index